Investing in the Metaverse

Advanced Strategies for Building a Web3 Portfolio Across Crypto, NFTs, DAOs, and Digital Assets

By Joe Correa

Published by Live Stronger Faster

This book is for educational and informational purposes only. The author and publisher are not engaged in rendering legal, financial, or other professional advice. Readers should consult a qualified professional before making any financial decisions.

First Edition

Table of Contents

Introduction

The metaverse has progressed far beyond an abstract concept, a buzzword, or a futuristic dream. It is no longer a playful experiment reserved for game developers, crypto enthusiasts, or Silicon Valley futurists; it has become a full-fledged economic ecosystem—one with financial rules, market dynamics, asset classes, and investment strategies that mirror and sometimes outperform the physical world. As we enter this final book of the *Metaverse Masterclass*, you are stepping into a world where wealth is generated not by physical constraints or traditional gatekeepers, but by digital ownership, borderless marketplaces, programmable assets, and global participation. You are entering a financial frontier still in its infancy—one that rewards early adopters, strategic thinkers, innovators, and those willing to see opportunity before the masses recognize its value. Book 10 is your guide to investing wisely, profitably, and sustainably in this new digital world.

This introduction begins by reframing what "investing" means in the context of Web3. In the traditional world, investing typically refers to stocks, real estate, bonds, commodities, or private businesses. But in the metaverse, investing expands into an entirely new universe of possibilities—cryptocurrencies, NFTs, virtual land, digital identity assets, tokenized communities, DAOs, metaverse startups, yield-generating platforms, fractionalized investments, AI-driven digital businesses, and more. While some of these assets behave similarly to traditional investments, others follow unique patterns, influenced by network effects, community adoption, tokenomics, platform utility, decentralization, and technological innovation. Instead of simply picking assets and hoping for upward price movements, successful metaverse investors understand ecosystems, incentives, user behavior, platform design, and macro trends in digital culture. This book will teach you how to navigate these complexities with clarity and confidence.

To truly understand metaverse investing, you must begin with the global shift that made it possible: the transition from Web2 to Web3. In Web2, users create value but platforms capture it. Your posts fuel engagement, your videos fuel algorithms, your activity fuels shareholder profit—but you own none of the value you create. Web3 reverses this relationship by introducing ownership into the internet. Whether it's holding digital land, buying part of a virtual business, participating in new token economies, or earning yield for contributing to decentralized networks, Web3 positions users not as consumers, but as owners. This change is monumental because it transforms every online action into a potential income stream or investment opportunity. The more time people spend in virtual worlds, the more valuable digital assets become. This is the core foundation of metaverse investing.

Investing in the metaverse is about understanding digital value—how it is created, how it grows, how it multiplies, and how it can be owned. It's also about recognizing that digital scarcity is real, community trust is an asset, and technological adoption curves can outperform any traditional market cycle. In virtual worlds, a digital property next to a popular event space can appreciate in value just like a physical home near an entertainment district. A rare NFT with cultural significance can become a digital blue-chip asset. A DAO token tied to a profitable virtual business can generate dividends. A game-based economy can produce real-world income. These aren't hypothetical scenarios; they are happening today. And as the digital population grows, so does the investment opportunity.

But every new economic frontier also presents risks—volatility, scams, emotional trading, speculative hype, project failure, regulatory uncertainty, and market cycles that move at the speed of the internet. This introduction is not about avoiding risks entirely—that is impossible in any investment space—but about equipping you with the knowledge to recognize them, manage them, and use them to your advantage. The metaverse favors educated participants, not gamblers. It rewards those who understand fundamental value, long-term strategy, and sustainable ecosystem growth. Throughout this book, you'll learn frameworks and systems that professional investors, hedge funds, and early Web3 pioneers use to evaluate opportunities and build resilient portfolios.

One of the most compelling aspects of metaverse investing is diversification, not simply between assets but across entirely different digital economies. You can hold cryptocurrency for liquidity and long-term appreciation. You can buy NFTs that represent ownership of unique digital items, art, identity, or intellectual property. You can invest in virtual land and build rental income streams or businesses. You can buy governance tokens and shape the direction of decentralized organizations. You can allocate capital into metaverse startups, gaming ecosystems, AI-powered digital assets, and tokenized marketplaces. In other words, you can build a financial empire that exists entirely online—an empire that never closes, never sleeps, and is accessible to anyone with an internet connection. This is democratized investing at its highest level.

In this introduction, it's important to recognize that the metaverse is not a single platform or virtual world—it is an interconnected network of digital spaces, economies, and experiences. Platforms may rise and fall, but the underlying shift toward digital ownership will remain. That's why this book will teach you principles, not just platforms. When you understand token value, digital scarcity, utility layers, community adoption, economic incentives, and platform risk, you will be able to evaluate any metaverse investment opportunity—even those that haven't been invented yet. You will not depend on hype cycles because you'll know how to analyze real value. You will not depend on luck because you'll know how to measure risk. You will not depend on guesses because you'll have strategies grounded in data, history, and economic psychology.

As we step into the chapters ahead, you will explore advanced strategies for building a Web3 portfolio that's diversified, income-producing, and future-proof. You'll learn how to identify undervalued crypto assets, evaluate NFT projects beyond surface-level art, assess virtual land deals with real estate principles, invest in DAOs strategically, participate in decentralized finance for yield, and build digital assets that appreciate over time. You'll also learn how to navigate bear markets, capitalize on bull markets, manage risk with precision, and maintain emotional discipline in the fast-moving world of Web3. By the end of this book, you won't just understand metaverse investing—you'll be able to build a portfolio designed for long-term wealth, passive income, and exponential upside.

The metaverse is not simply a trend. It is a digital transformation shaping the next era of human interaction, creativity, commerce, and ownership. And investors who understand it now—during its early and volatile stages—will be the ones who reap the greatest rewards. This book is your final step in the Metaverse Masterclass, but in many ways, it is also the beginning of your journey as a digital investor and pioneer. Welcome to Book 10. Welcome to the frontier of Web3 wealth. The metaverse is expanding, the opportunities are multiplying, and your role as an investor starts now.

Chapter 1

The Foundations of Metaverse Investing: Understanding Digital Value, Ownership, and Opportunity

Before you can build a profitable metaverse investment portfolio, you must deeply understand the mechanics that make digital assets valuable. The metaverse is not built on speculation alone, nor is it sustained by hype cycles or temporary market excitement. Instead, its investment landscape is powered by a combination of technology, human behavior, decentralization, digital ownership rights, and the network effects that form new economic ecosystems. To become a strategic and profitable Web3 investor, you must master these fundamentals. Without this foundation, every investment you make will be based on surface-level assumptions instead of structural understanding. Chapter 1 lays the groundwork by revealing the essential pillars of metaverse investing—pillars that will guide every decision you make throughout this book.

The first foundational element is **digital ownership**, which became possible only through blockchain technology. Prior to blockchain, anything digital could be copied endlessly without proof of origin or verification of true ownership. This made digital scarcity—and by extension, digital value—impossible. Blockchain changed everything by introducing an immutable ledger that proves who owns what, when they acquired it, and the entire chain of custody. In the traditional world, we rely on governments, banks, or institutions to maintain these records. In Web3, the blockchain does it automatically, transparently, and without centralized control. This shift enables new types of digital assets—cryptocurrencies, NFTs, virtual land, tokenized businesses, DAO shares, metaverse identities—and each one represents a form of provable, portable, programmable ownership. Understanding ownership is the key to understanding value.

The second foundational element is **digital scarcity**, the mechanism that limits the supply of an asset and allows demand to influence price. Bitcoin introduced the world to controlled digital scarcity by capping supply at 21 million coins. NFTs introduced uniqueness—each token is distinct, and no two are identical unless designed that way. Virtual land introduced limited digital geography inside virtual worlds, creating demand based on digital "location," foot traffic, platform growth, and social visibility. Scarcity does not artificially inflate value; rather, it provides the conditions for value creation. In metaverse investing, scarcity is a tool—one that helps you identify which assets have durable long-term potential and which are simply unlimited commodities.

The third foundational element is **utility**, or the usefulness of the asset within its ecosystem. In traditional investing, utility might be represented by dividends, cash flow, rights, services, or real-world use cases. In the metaverse, utility is even more diverse: governance capabilities, voting rights, staking opportunities, exclusive access, in-game power, digital identity benefits, brand building tools, or opportunities for yield. Investors who buy NFTs solely for artwork often misunderstand the deeper value: access to communities, tools, education, events, metaverse experiences, partnerships, or even profit-sharing mechanisms. Utility is what separates long-term investments from temporary fads. When evaluating any metaverse asset, ask yourself: “What does this unlock for me? What does it allow me to do, become, or build?”

The fourth foundation is **network value**, driven by adoption and community participation. In Web3, the value of an asset often grows not because of its intrinsic characteristics, but because of the strength, size, and loyalty of its user base. A cryptocurrency with powerful evangelists can outperform a technically superior coin with weak community support. A metaverse platform with active participants can generate higher land values than one with better graphics but fewer users. An NFT project with passionate believers can sustain long-term cultural value. Network value is the fuel behind viral growth, ecosystem resilience, and appreciation. As an investor, you must learn to measure community strength: activity, transparency, leadership, communication, developer engagement, and retention. Communities are the "moats" that protect Web3 projects from collapse.

The fifth foundational element is **tokenomics**, the economic design behind how tokens are created, distributed, incentivized, and managed. Tokenomics determines how supply enters the market, how rewards are issued, how inflation occurs, how deflationary mechanisms work, and how incentives shape user behavior. Good tokenomics motivate healthy participation and long-term sustainability. Poor tokenomics create price crashes, ecosystem collapse, or runaway inflation. Investors must analyze distribution schedules, treasury allocations, founder vesting periods, burn mechanisms, staking rewards, and governance systems. Tokenomics is the economic engine of the metaverse—learn it, and you gain predictive insight into the future of an asset.

The sixth foundation is **interoperability**, the ability of assets to move across platforms, wallets, chains, or metaverse worlds. Assets that can travel, integrate, and remain usable across multiple ecosystems tend to hold stronger long-term value because they are not tied to the survival of a single platform. Interoperability also expands use cases, enhances liquidity, and reduces risk. As an investor, assets that are portable across chains and environments are generally more protective during market volatility. Understanding interoperability helps you identify which metaverse platforms may survive, merge, evolve, or become dominant.

The seventh foundational element is **behavioral economics**—the emotional and psychological patterns that drive human decision-making in the metaverse economy. Fear of missing out, panic selling, overconfidence, tribalism, social proof, hype, and digital culture influence prices more than traditional fundamentals. Successful Web3 investors understand these dynamics and remain emotionally neutral. Instead of chasing trends, they analyze sentiment, cycles, catalysts, and macro conditions. They protect themselves from euphoria and fear. They plan their entries and exits logically. In the metaverse, your success is determined as much by emotional discipline as by technical knowledge.

Finally, the eighth foundational element is **macro Web3 adoption trends**, including global regulation, institutional participation, gaming expansion, VR/AR improvements, interoperability standards, cultural shifts toward digital identity, and the corporate entry into virtual worlds. These macro trends form the context in which metaverse investments rise and fall. When adoption accelerates, asset values rise. When regulatory uncertainty increases, prices may contract. Understanding macro forces helps you make rational decisions and position yourself for future opportunities.

These foundations form the pillars of metaverse investing. Together, they create a mental model that allows you to evaluate any digital asset—new, old, large, small, speculative, or stable. Mastering these pillars gives you the ability to think like an early-stage investor, analyze like a strategist, and act like a long-term builder. As you progress through this book, these foundations will anchor every strategy, framework, and decision you make. They are your compass inside the Web3 economy and the roadmap for building wealth in the metaverse for years to come.

"The Investor of Two Worlds"

Aiden had always been fascinated by technology, but nothing intrigued him more than the idea of a world where value wasn't limited by borders, buildings, or even physical reality. He had made a modest living trading stocks and crypto, but he knew something was missing—the opportunity to get in early on the next major economic frontier. One night, while scrolling through online forums, he stumbled upon a headline that stopped him cold: "Virtual Land Sale Generates $2.4 Million in a Single Day." His first instinct was disbelief. How could land that didn't physically exist be worth millions? But curiosity pulled him deeper.

The next morning, he joined a virtual world for the first time. When the loading screen faded, Aiden found himself standing in a city that wasn't real—yet felt more alive than anywhere he had been online. Neon signs flickered above futuristic stores, avatars walked past him with purpose, music echoed from a digital plaza, and floating billboards advertised metaverse concerts, NFT galleries, and virtual casinos. It was overwhelming, yet exhilarating. It felt like stepping into a new universe—one where the rules hadn't been written yet.

Aiden wandered through streets of digital skyscrapers until he reached a quiet rooftop overlooking the city. A sign glowed in the distance: *"Own Your Piece of the Future."* He couldn't shake the feeling that this wasn't just a game—it was a new economy forming in real time. He met an older avatar nearby, a calm and confident figure named Nova. She appeared experienced, wearing gear that looked rare and valuable. Without turning, she asked, "First time here?" Aiden nodded. Nova said, "Then let me teach you how this world really works."

She explained digital ownership, how blockchain made it possible for someone to truly own land, art, items, identities, or businesses inside a virtual world. She compared it to real-world deeds and titles, but without government dependency. “Ownership is freedom,” she said. “It’s power. It’s opportunity.” They teleported to a digital gallery where each NFT had its own story, history, and price. Aiden realized that he wasn’t just looking at pictures—he was looking at verifiable assets with unique value.

Nova guided him next to a land hub where plots were being bought and sold. She showed him scarcity maps, development plans, traffic projections, and community proposals. “Just like in the real world,” she said, “location matters. Scarcity matters. Adoption matters.” Aiden felt his mind opening to a new way of thinking. This wasn’t fantasy—it was economics, psychology, and technology combined.

They traveled to a DAO headquarters floating in the sky. Hundreds of voices echoed as members voted on proposals. Nova explained tokenomics, community strength, and interoperability. She emphasized emotional discipline, how fear and excitement could push investors into mistakes. Aiden listened closely. He realized that this new world behaved like the physical world—but moved ten times faster.

Hours passed as they visited thriving districts and failed projects. Nova showed him communities that collapsed due to poor token design and others that grew because of strong leadership and utility. Finally, they returned to the rooftop where they started. The sun was rising over the digital horizon—an artificial sunrise that somehow felt symbolic. Aiden asked, "Why teach me all this?" Nova smiled. "Because every investor has two worlds now—the physical one and the digital one. The ones who understand both will create the future."

Aiden logged off, his heart racing. He knew he had witnessed the early stages of something massive. This wasn't a game. It was the next frontier of wealth. And he intended to become one of the pioneers who mastered it. The journey ahead would require discipline, knowledge, and courage—but he felt ready. He had one foot in the real world and one in the metaverse, and for the first time in his life, he felt like he was standing exactly where he belonged.

Chapter 2

Evaluating Metaverse Investments: Frameworks, Metrics, and Analysis Models Used by Professional Web3 Investors

Now that you understand the foundations of digital value, it's time to learn how professional metaverse investors actually evaluate opportunities. While many newcomers buy assets based on hype, emotion, or the influence of social media, experienced Web3 investors use structured frameworks rooted in data, psychology, economics, and long-term ecosystem analysis. Chapter 2 provides the complete evaluation system used by venture capitalists, Web3 analysts, and crypto-native investors to determine which metaverse assets deserve capital—and which should be avoided. The goal is not to eliminate risk, because risk is inherent in early-stage digital economies. The goal is to apply the right analytical lens to maximize upside while minimizing exposure to asset failure. This chapter gives you the tools to do exactly that.

The first step in evaluating a metaverse investment is to analyze the **project vision and problem-solving narrative**. Every successful digital asset solves a problem, fills a gap, or creates an opportunity. A cryptocurrency might solve an issue in payments or decentralization. A virtual land platform might address digital community building or identity expression. An NFT collection might serve as a membership system for creators. A DAO token might democratize decision-making. By understanding the problem a project claims to solve, you can immediately gauge whether its value proposition is compelling and necessary. Weak projects typically offer vague promises like "changing the future" or "bringing people together," while strong projects deliver clear, specific, and practical solutions. Ask yourself: Does this asset have a reason to exist, or is it simply capitalizing on hype?

The second step is evaluating the **team**, one of the strongest predictors of long-term survival. A strong team may include experienced developers, game designers, blockchain architects, brand builders, economists, marketers, or entrepreneurs with prior wins. In Web3, anonymous founders can succeed, but they must demonstrate transparency, consistent communication, and a clear track record of delivering results. Teams that disappear for weeks, fail to update roadmaps, or constantly promise future announcements are red flags. Professional investors study how founders speak, how they respond to challenges, and how well they execute. Vision matters, but execution determines survival. The third element of evaluation is **technology and**

infrastructure quality. For metaverse platforms, this includes graphics engines, scalability, user interface, interoperability, performance, world-building tools, programming layers, and asset portability. For cryptocurrencies, it includes consensus mechanisms, security, scalability, decentralization, and developer ecosystem support. For NFTs, it includes smart contract quality, metadata structure, utility layers, and storage protocols. Many projects collapse simply because their technology cannot handle user growth. Evaluate whether the technology is robust, future-proof, and adaptable.

The fourth evaluation pillar is **ecosystem demand**, which reflects how many users actually want what the project offers. This is where network effects become critical. You must study user activity, community enthusiasm, developer contribution, social engagement, and the rate at which new users join the ecosystem. Demand is not measured by hype or social media followers. It is measured by **behavior**—how often people use the product, how long they stay engaged, how much they build on top of it, and how much value flows through the ecosystem. Strong projects show consistent daily engagement, not just spikes during marketing campaigns.

The fifth framework is analyzing **tokenomics**. Professional investors study supply constraints, token distribution schedules, founder vesting periods, staking incentives, utility design, deflationary mechanisms, inflation risks, treasury management, and governance structures. Tokenomics shape the entire economy of a metaverse asset. Poor tokenomics—like limitless supply, high inflation, low utility, or unfair founder allocations—make long-term appreciation difficult. Strong tokenomics align user behavior with ecosystem growth and reward participation. This chapter emphasizes that tokenomics can make or break a project, even if everything else looks promising.

The sixth component is **competitive advantage and differentiation**. The metaverse is crowded, and many platforms attempt to copy successful models. Investors must identify what makes a project defensible. Is it brand recognition? A unique economic model? Established partnerships? A first-mover advantage? Exclusive intellectual property? Strong interoperability? A powerful creator ecosystem? A moat separates long-term winners from short-lived imitators. If a project can easily be copied, its future value is weak. If it has defensibility, it can dominate its niche.

Next, you must evaluate **monetization models**. How does the project generate revenue? How will it sustain itself? For platforms, this could include transaction fees, land sales, royalties, subscriptions, or in-world commerce. For NFTs, it may include membership revenue, utility upgrades, or licensing. For DAOs, it may be treasury growth, yield strategies, or protocol fees. Projects without clear monetization eventually rely on new user growth, which is unsustainable. Sustainable revenue is the backbone of long-term asset appreciation.

Another critical factor is **liquidity and market health**. Investors analyze trading volume, liquidity depth, exchange availability, and buying/selling friction. Even strong assets can be risky if liquidity is thin, because it's difficult to exit positions without affecting price. Healthy liquidity signals strong market confidence and investor participation. Assets with high volatility but low liquidity are especially dangerous for new investors.

The final evaluation category is **risk profiling**. Investors assess project maturity, regulatory uncertainty, team transparency, technology vulnerabilities, market volatility, ecosystem fragility, and competition threats. They categorize assets into high, medium, or low risk and allocate capital accordingly. Professional investors rarely overexpose themselves to a single asset, even if the potential upside is significant. This discipline protects them during market downturns and positions them for long-term wins.

When combined, these frameworks form the complete evaluation system for metaverse investment. They allow you to analyze any asset objectively—whether it is a cryptocurrency, NFT collection, metaverse platform, virtual land project, or DAO token. By using these frameworks consistently, you begin thinking like a Web3 analyst, not a speculator. You stop chasing pumps and start identifying real value. You stop relying on hype and start relying on fundamentals. You stop gambling and start investing with strategy, purpose, and long-term foresight.

"The Blueprint of Value"

Aiden sat at his desk, staring at his laptop screen as hundreds of Web3 projects flashed before his eyes. Some promised the future of gaming, some offered "life-changing" NFTs, and others claimed to revolutionize digital identity. It was overwhelming. He wanted to invest, but he didn't know how to separate real opportunity from polished scams. Nova's lessons from their rooftop meeting replayed in his mind. She had shown him the foundations, but now he needed to learn how to evaluate projects like a professional.

A notification pinged. Nova invited him to a private analysis session inside a virtual research hub—an elevated observatory floating above the metaverse city. Aiden entered the portal. The room around him transformed into a vaulted chamber filled with holographic displays, charts, and glowing orbs representing different Web3 projects. Nova floated slightly above the ground, as usual, calm and confident. “Welcome,” she said. “Tonight, we study the blueprint of value.”

She pointed toward the first hologram—a metaverse platform claiming to be the “future of digital living.” It looked impressive, but Nova zoomed in on the founding team’s history. There was almost nothing there. No track record, no communication, no real leadership. “Many investors jump in because the marketing is flashy,” she said. “But a weak team is like building a skyscraper on sand.” Aiden nodded. He had invested in a few crypto tokens like that in the past—and watched them collapse.

Next, she opened a visualization of another project—this one with a clear, compelling problem it aimed to solve: secure identity verification across virtual worlds. The founders had built successful tech start-ups before. Their roadmap was practical and detailed. “Strong vision,” Nova said. “Strong team. Strong foundation. This is what value looks like.” Aiden realized how different this project felt. There was purpose and structure behind it.

The observatory shifted to display a grid of virtual land plots glowing in different colors. Nova said, “This map shows demand." The brightest areas represented platform zones with heavy user activity. The darkest zones represented abandoned developments. "Some investors buy land anywhere and expect profits. Professionals understand ecosystems." She teleported Aiden to a thriving district filled with creators, shops, galleries, and events. The energy was electric. Then she teleported him to a silent, empty district. It looked like a ghost town. "Same platform," she said. "Different outcomes. Demand is everything."

Next, she brought him to a circular arena where floating tokens rotated around a large economic engine. "Tokenomics," she said. "The heartbeat of Web3 economies." She showed him a token with unlimited supply that increased daily—its inflation made it nearly worthless. Then she showed him one with a carefully balanced supply, staking incentives, burn mechanisms, and governance rights. "Good tokenomics create sustainable ecosystems," Nova explained. "Bad tokenomics destroy them."

Aiden followed as she moved to a holographic display comparing a dozen NFT projects. Some had beautiful artwork but no utility. Others offered tools, membership access, education portals, and partnerships. "Utility," she said. "Most people ignore it. But it determines whether an asset lives or dies." Aiden examined one NFT collection with a robust creator ecosystem and a roadmap for future use cases. He felt that spark inside him—the feeling of spotting real potential. The final part of the session took place in a virtual war room where Nova laid out rows of risk profiles. She explained how seasoned investors assess liquidity, volatility, competition, and regulatory concerns. She showed charts of projects that surged then collapsed, not because they were bad ideas, but because investors ignored warning signs. "Every asset carries risk," Nova said. "But smart investors prepare for it. They allocate wisely. They diversify. They stay disciplined."

As the session ended, Aiden felt transformed. He understood now that the metaverse wasn't chaos—it was a system. It had patterns, structures, and signals. You just needed the right lens to see them. Nova placed a glowing chip in his hand. "This is your analysis key," she said. "It anchors the frameworks we studied. Use it whenever you evaluate new opportunities." Aiden felt its energy pulse. It wasn't magic—it was a reminder that knowledge, not luck, would define his success.

When he logged off, Aiden felt clarity for the first time since entering Web3. The metaverse wasn't a mystery anymore. It was a blueprint waiting to be understood. And he finally had the tools to read it.

Chapter 3

Building a Diversified Metaverse Portfolio: Crypto, NFTs, Virtual Land, Tokens, DAOs, and Digital Businesses

Diversification is the cornerstone of intelligent investing—not just in the stock market, but especially in the metaverse. Web3 assets behave differently from anything in traditional finance. They are influenced by cultural shifts, technological adoption, digital scarcity, community engagement, economic incentives, and rapid innovation cycles. Because of that, concentrating your capital in a single asset class dramatically increases risk. The metaverse rewards those who build portfolios across multiple categories—cryptocurrency, NFTs, virtual real estate, DAO tokens, gaming assets, and digital businesses. Chapter 3 shows you how professionals structure diversified metaverse portfolios that can withstand volatility while capturing exponential upside.

The first major category is **cryptocurrency**, the backbone of the entire Web3 ecosystem. Cryptocurrencies serve as money, fuel, governance, infrastructure, and the settlement layer for digital commerce. They are often the most liquid assets in a Web3 portfolio, making them ideal for both long-term growth and strategic rebalancing. A diversified crypto allocation typically includes foundational layer-1 assets like Ethereum, Solana, or Avalanche; layer-2 scaling solutions; gaming coins; and AI-powered tokens. The goal is not to gamble on small coins but to establish strong exposure to the infrastructure powering the digital economy. While these assets can be volatile, they also tend to recover strongest during market upcycles because they enable the entire metaverse to function.

The second portfolio category is **NFTs**, which represent ownership of unique digital items. NFTs are not simply collectibles; they are identity assets, technology assets, brand assets, utility passes, creator tools, and digital ownership certificates. When evaluating NFTs for diversification, investors often break them into categories such as blue-chip collections with long-term cultural relevance, utility NFTs that unlock tools or income, membership NFTs that grant access to communities, game-based NFTs with in-world value, and intellectual property NFTs with licensing potential. A diversified NFT allocation avoids overexposure to hype and instead focuses on utility, community strength, adoption, and historical significance. NFTs behave differently from tokens—they are illiquid, influenced by culture, and tightly tied to community sentiment. That's why they require thoughtful allocation and long-term conviction. The third category is **virtual land**, one of the fastest-growing asset classes in digital real estate. In the physical world, real estate investing is limited by geography, regulation, and capital requirements. In the metaverse, land is accessible globally, permissionless, and often inexpensive compared to physical property. Virtual land generates income through renting, advertising, hosting events, building stores, or creating digital experiences. It appreciates based on platform adoption, foot traffic, creator presence, and digital zoning. A diversified approach to virtual land investing involves spreading holdings across multiple metaverse platforms to reduce platform-specific risk. You also want exposure to different use cases—commercial districts, creator hubs, gaming environments, entertainment zones, and community-driven lands. Like physical real estate, digital property rewards patience and strategic development.

The fourth category is **DAO tokens**, which represent voting rights, governance influence, and sometimes profit participation in decentralized communities. DAOs behave like digital cooperatives—users contribute to the ecosystem and earn voting power. Some DAOs manage multimillion-dollar treasuries, invest in startups, build software, or run virtual worlds. A well-diversified metaverse portfolio includes governance tokens that grant access to decision-making in strong communities. DAO tokens can appreciate significantly when the DAO executes successful initiatives, forms powerful partnerships, or innovates within the ecosystem. But they also carry risk, because poor governance can collapse a project. That's why investors must diversify across multiple DAOs with different missions, growth paths, and user bases.

The fifth category is **gaming assets**, which include in-game currencies, rare items, characters, skins, weapons, vehicles, and other assets that hold value inside virtual worlds. These assets often appreciate based on player adoption, game updates, tournament activity, and ecosystem health. Professional investors include gaming assets in their portfolios because gaming drives much of the metaverse's cultural momentum. It attracts millions of users, fuels creator economies, and accelerates digital identity adoption. Diversification across gaming ecosystems reduces risk in case one game loses popularity or fails to scale.

The sixth category is **digital businesses**, one of the most underrated forms of metaverse investment. A digital business can be a virtual store, an in-world event space, a metaverse consulting service, a digital product brand, a creator studio, a virtual rental business, or an experience-driven company that earns tokens and fees. These businesses produce income, not just appreciation. They can scale globally, run autonomously, and operate 24/7. Including digital business exposure in your portfolio stabilizes returns during bear markets and multiplies gains during bull markets. Another key diversification component involves **exposure across risk levels**. This means having a mix of high, medium, and low-risk assets. Blue-chip crypto and established NFTs offer stability. Mid-tier altcoins, growing DAOs, or virtual land in emerging platforms offer medium risk with high upside. Early-stage gaming projects, small collections, or new DAOs offer high risk but explosive potential. A well-balanced portfolio spreads risk while allowing exposure to category winners—the assets that can generate exponential returns.

Finally, diversification includes **time span diversification**, meaning you invest with different timelines in mind—short-term plays, medium-term holds, and long-term conviction assets. The metaverse moves fast, but long-term winners emerge through cycles. By diversifying across timelines, you protect yourself from liquidity traps, emotional trading, and market downturns.

A diversified metaverse portfolio is more than a collection of assets—it is an adaptive ecosystem designed to thrive in a rapidly evolving world. By combining different asset classes, risk levels, timelines, and use cases, you create resilience, protect capital, and maximize upside. Diversification is the difference between surviving the digital frontier and mastering it.

"The Map of Many Worlds"

Aiden returned to the metaverse city with a new mission: building his first real investment portfolio. Nova had taught him the foundations and shown him how to evaluate projects, but now he wanted to learn how professionals structured their portfolios. As he entered the main plaza, he found Nova waiting beside a glowing portal shaped like a compass. "Today," she said, "you learn the importance of mapping your investments across many worlds."

They stepped into the portal and emerged inside a massive floating sphere filled with miniature holographic planets—each spinning with glowing symbols representing different asset classes. Nova gestured to the first planet, a bright and fiery orb pulsing with energy. "Crypto," she said. "The power cores of the metaverse." As the planet rotated, Aiden saw tiny rivers of light flowing across its surface—the blockchain networks that powered every world. Nova zoomed in, showing him Ethereum like a city of glowing towers, Solana as a fast-moving grid of light, and other chains expanding outward. "These are the roots," she explained. "Without them, nothing else grows."

They moved to the next planet—a radiant sphere covered in intricate patterns. "NFTs," Nova said. "These are identities, memberships, tools, experiences, and access." Aiden watched thousands of symbols float across the planet's oceans of color.

Each represented a digital item with unique ownership and utility. Some glowed brightly with strong communities behind them, while others flickered weakly, fading from existence. "Choose NFTs with purpose," Nova advised. "Not just beauty."

The third planet was vast, with shimmering landmasses floating atop holographic water. "Virtual land," she said. "Digital real estate." As they hovered above the world, Aiden saw bustling districts filled with creators, stores, concerts, and events. Then he saw empty zones where abandoned projects once thrived. "Land grows with communities," she said. "Healthy cities attract value. Empty ones decay." Aiden imagined owning property here, renting it to creators, hosting events, or building experiences. The potential felt endless.

The fourth planet was a glowing council chamber in the sky. Tokens hovered like floating flames. "DAOs," Nova said. "Communities governed by their members." Inside, Aiden saw hundreds of avatars debating proposals, casting votes, and directing multi-million-dollar treasuries. Some DAOs looked organized and purposeful. Others felt chaotic and directionless. "DAOs are powerful," she warned, "but power requires structure."

The next planet spun rapidly, filled with moving images, characters, weapons, ships, and mythical creatures. "Gaming assets," Nova said. "They rise and fall with cultures and trends." Aiden saw tournaments, battles, adventures, and players trading items with real value. "Some games become universes," Nova said. "Others fade. That is why you diversify."

Finally, they arrived at the sixth planet—a pulsing metropolis made entirely of neon light. Digital storefronts, creative studios, event spaces, consulting hubs, and automation businesses filled every corner. "Digital businesses," she explained. "These produce income, not just appreciation. They create stability during chaos." Aiden felt drawn to this planet. It represented entrepreneurship in its purest form—building something inside a world with no limits.

Nova summoned all six planets into alignment. They formed a constellation around Aiden, each glowing with equal intensity. "A single asset makes you vulnerable," she said. "A diversified portfolio makes you unstoppable." She touched each planet, causing them to collapse into six glowing shards floating in her hand. Then she placed them in Aiden's chest. They sank into him like warm light. "These are your worlds now," she said. "Your task is to balance them with wisdom."

Aiden felt the shards inside him—crypto's power, NFTs' identity, land's stability, DAOs' influence, gaming's culture, and digital business' income potential. For the first time, he felt like a true investor, not a spectator. He looked at Nova. “What happens next?” She smiled. “Next, you learn how to build strategies that turn diversification into wealth.”

Aiden knew his journey had just begun. But now he had a map—a map of many worlds—and he felt ready to explore every one of them.

Chapter 4

How to Identify High-Value Crypto Assets for Long-Term Metaverse Investing

Cryptocurrency remains the core investment vehicle of the metaverse. While NFTs, DAOs, virtual land, and digital businesses all play critical roles, cryptocurrencies form the infrastructure that allows everything else to function. They provide the money, the settlement layers, the governance frameworks, the security, and the computational resources powering the decentralized digital world. Because of this foundational importance, identifying high-value crypto assets is one of the most profitable skills an investor can develop. Chapter 4 unveils the analytical frameworks used by elite Web3 investors to identify cryptocurrencies with real long-term potential—assets capable of surviving cycles, powering entire economies, and delivering exponential returns.

The first principle in evaluating high-value crypto assets is understanding **their role in the ecosystem**. Cryptocurrencies are not all the same—some serve as money, others act as infrastructure, others govern networks, and others power applications. Layer-1 blockchains like Ethereum, Solana, Avalanche, NEAR, and Aptos act like digital nations with their own economies, infrastructure, and developer populations. Layer-2 solutions provide scalability and lower fees, enabling mass adoption. Application-specific tokens fuel gaming ecosystems, social protocols, and decentralized services. Governance tokens allow holders to vote on platform decisions. Understanding the asset's role determines whether it has fundamental demand. High-value crypto assets typically play essential roles that other tokens depend on, making them foundational rather than optional.

The second principle is analyzing **adoption and network usage**. Real adoption is visible through transaction volume, active users, daily wallet activity, developer engagement, and ecosystem growth. Strong networks show consistent usage even during market downturns. They have diverse communities, multiple applications, growing developer tools, and expanding infrastructure. Metrics such as TVL (total value locked), NFT marketplace activity, staking participation, and cross-chain bridges provide additional insight into whether a network is gaining or losing strength. The most valuable assets in the metaverse are those with thriving ecosystems—not those that rely solely on marketing hype.

The third principle is studying **developer momentum**, which is one of the strongest predictors of long-term viability. A blockchain with a fast-growing developer ecosystem will likely innovate, expand its capabilities, and attract high-quality applications. Investors should monitor developer conferences, GitHub activity, grants, hackathons, and partnerships. Developer engagement indicates confidence in the chain's technology, tools, and long-term potential. Historically, chains with strong developer communities become dominant—even if they face early challenges or temporary setbacks.

The fourth principle is analyzing **scalability and performance**. High-value crypto assets must support thousands or millions of users without sacrificing security or decentralization. Investors evaluate transaction capacity, fees, speed, energy consumption, consensus mechanisms, and upgrade roadmaps. Assets that solve scalability without compromising security are positioned to become long-term infrastructure for the metaverse. Investors must also understand the trade-offs of each chain—some prioritize decentralization, others prioritize speed, and others focus on adaptability. The strongest assets find balance or evolve toward it.

The fifth principle is understanding **tokenomics**, especially supply dynamics. High-value cryptocurrencies often have capped or controlled supply, deflationary mechanisms, staking rewards aligned with utility, and fair distribution models. Investors avoid assets with unlimited supply inflation, unfair token allocations, or short-term reward structures that dilute value. Tokenomics influence everything: adoption, investor participation, network security, and price appreciation. Strong tokenomics attract long-term holders and discourage speculative dumping.

The sixth principle is examining **governance strength**, especially for networks governed by token holders. Effective governance ensures that the network can adapt to technological trends, fix issues, develop upgrades, and respond to economic or cultural shifts. Weak governance slows innovation, causes internal conflict, and can destroy promising projects. Strong governance results in faster upgrades, clearer long-term vision, and stable leadership. Investors must evaluate how community decisions are made, how transparent voting processes are, and how effectively past decisions have improved the network.

Another critical factor is **partnerships and institutional confidence**. High-value crypto assets often form alliances with major companies, infrastructure providers, universities, governments, or global brands. These partnerships bring credibility, resources, and adoption. Institutional backing signals trust in the asset's long-term viability. Investors should monitor ecosystem announcements, enterprise integrations, and collaborations with real-world industries like gaming, finance, entertainment, and virtual experiences.

The eighth principle is assessing **cultural relevance**, which is surprisingly powerful in Web3. Some cryptocurrencies become cultural movements—symbols of decentralization, innovation, or rebellion. These narratives create loyalty, evangelism, and sustained demand. Culturally strong assets maintain relevance even during downturns because users believe in their identity and mission. While cultural momentum cannot replace fundamentals, it significantly enhances them.

Finally, investors must evaluate the asset's **resilience across market cycles**. High-value cryptocurrencies recover faster after crashes, maintain community strength during bear markets, and grow during consolidation phases. Studying past cycles reveals which assets have real staying power and which were temporary hype. Long-term investors prioritize resilience because assets that survive multiple cycles tend to become the giants of the next era.

When combined, these principles allow investors to identify crypto assets capable of shaping the digital future. High-value cryptocurrencies are not defined by price, hype, or short-term pumps. They are defined by adoption, infrastructure strength, community loyalty, developer momentum, and economic design. By mastering these evaluation principles, you can build a crypto foundation that supports your entire metaverse portfolio—now and for decades to come.

"The Engines Beneath the World"

Aiden returned to the metaverse the way a pilot returns to a familiar sky—excited, determined, and ready to explore another layer of this digital universe. Nova greeted him outside a towering structure that stretched into the clouds, its metallic walls humming with energy. "This," she said, "is the Hall of Engines. Every world you've visited runs on power from here."

Aiden followed her inside. The hall opened into an endless chamber filled with massive floating machines—each a swirling engine of light representing a different blockchain network. Some engines pulsed steadily like beating hearts. Others flickered erratically. A few burned with almost blinding brilliance. Nova pointed to the largest engine, an intricate machine of shifting geometric shapes. "This is Ethereum," she said. "One of the original engines of the metaverse." Aiden watched as streams of data flowed through it like rivers, connecting hundreds of smaller engines throughout the chamber.

"This entire world depends on engines like these," Nova explained. "They provide security, speed, structure, and trust." She waved her hand, and suddenly holograms appeared around the Ethereum engine—graphs showing user adoption, developer activity, staking participation, and network upgrades. "These metrics," she said, "are signs of a powerful engine. Healthy. Growing. Resilient."

Aiden nodded as they moved to the next engine. It was sleek and fast-moving, glowing with bright streaks of neon blue. "Solana," Nova said. "Built for speed." She showed him how this engine processed transactions rapidly, enabling games, markets, and high-demand applications. But she also pointed out when the engine had faltered in past cycles. "Every engine has strengths and weaknesses," she said. "Your job as an investor is to evaluate both."

They passed by newer engines—smaller but growing quickly, each with its own personality. Some were efficient and elegant. Some were rugged and battle-tested. Others were experimental, humming with potential but lacking stability. Nova explained developer engagement, showing Aiden how each engine attracted creators who built new applications, marketplaces, games, and financial tools. "Developers," she said, "are the lifeblood of an engine. Without them, even the brightest machines fade."

They reached a dark corner where engines flickered weakly. Some were barely lit. “These,” she said quietly, “are the failed worlds.” Aiden stepped closer. Each engine had once been full of hype—massive marketing, bold promises, huge communities. But now they were abandoned, silent, and rusting away. “They lacked real adoption,” Nova said. “Or strong leadership. Or solid tokenomics. Or governance. Many looked unstoppable in their prime, but they weren’t built to last.”

Aiden felt a chill as he stared at the remains of these collapsed projects. It reminded him of his own earlier mistakes—times he had invested based on excitement instead of knowledge. Nova placed a reassuring hand on his shoulder. “Failure teaches,” she said. “Resilience reveals truth.” She pointed to an engine that had dimmed during past downturns but now shined steadily once more. “The strongest assets survive cycles.”

They then traveled to the Council of Chains, a balcony overlooking thousands of engines. From here, Aiden could see which networks were growing, which were shrinking, and which were steady. Nova explained tokenomics as they watched supply mechanics, staking flows, and burn mechanisms visualized as living patterns of light. He saw deflationary tokens tightening their supply like contracting stars and inflationary tokens leaking energy with every cycle. Governance appeared as floating symbols representing votes and proposals—some well-coordinated, others chaotic. Then Nova activated a final visualization. A cascade of lights swept across the chamber, revealing how each engine connected to the next—cross-chain bridges, liquidity flows, application networks, and user migration patterns. Aiden saw the metaverse as a living ecosystem, its lifeblood flowing through these engines. He finally understood the bigger picture: crypto wasn't money. It was the power grid of the digital universe.

Nova turned to him and said, "If you can understand the engines, you can understand the future. Value begins here. Strength begins here. Wealth begins here."

Aiden felt the truth in her words. He wasn't just learning how to trade—he was learning how to read the pulse of an entire world. And as he left the Hall of Engines, he felt a new sense of clarity. The metaverse wasn't random or chaotic. It was powered by structures, networks, and forces that could be understood. And now, for the first time, he could see the engines beneath every digital world.

Chapter 5

Evaluating NFTs for Investment: Identifying High-Utility, High-Demand, and Long-Term Digital Assets

NFTs are one of the most misunderstood—and most potentially lucrative—asset classes in the metaverse. To beginners, NFTs often appear as simple digital images or collectibles. But to sophisticated Web3 investors, NFTs represent digital identity, access, utility, ownership, intellectual property, tokenized rights, and tradable assets with real-world earning potential. Evaluating NFTs properly requires going far deeper than artwork or hype. Chapter 5 teaches the full analytical system used by high-level NFT investors to distinguish valuable projects from short-lived trends.

The first critical principle is analyzing **utility**, which is the true engine of NFT value. Utility is anything the NFT allows you to do: gain access to private communities, unlock tools, receive educational resources, enter virtual events, claim future airdrops, earn staking rewards, license the artwork, participate in business networks, or access token-gated marketplaces. High-value NFTs deliver ongoing, evolving utility—not one-time benefits. When evaluating NFT utility, investors ask: Does the NFT unlock something useful? Does utility grow over time? Is it something people are willing to pay a premium for? Utility-based NFTs tend to survive market cycles because they provide ongoing value regardless of hype.

The second principle is assessing **community strength**, which is one of the most powerful indicators of long-term NFT value. The NFT market is driven heavily by culture, identity, and collective enthusiasm. Communities that are active, supportive, well-led, skilled, and self-sustaining create momentum that elevates the value of their assets. Strong communities participate in discussions, show up to events, contribute to development, and promote the ecosystem. Weak communities fade quickly. Investors examine engagement levels, leadership presence, communication quality, brand consistency, and the emotional tone of the community. A passionate, mission-driven community can support an NFT project for years—even decades.

The third principle is understanding **brand and cultural relevance**. Some NFTs become powerful cultural symbols—representations of digital identity, creativity, innovation, or status. These “blue-chip” NFTs often gain long-term value because they anchor themselves in history, adopt iconic styles, and represent milestones in digital culture.

Their value is supported not just by utility but by narrative. Investors study the uniqueness of the artwork, the story behind the project, the vision of the founders, and the position the NFT holds within the broader Web3 culture. NFTs with strong cultural relevance tend to appreciate steadily and hold value even during downturns.

The fourth principle is evaluating the **founding team**, which is as important for NFTs as it is for crypto projects. Strong NFT teams bring expertise in branding, art, technology, community management, game development, or Web3 entrepreneurship. They communicate transparently, deliver on roadmaps, and support their holders consistently. Weak teams hide behind anonymity, disappear after minting, or rely on buzzwords instead of execution. Investors examine past achievements, public visibility, partnerships, and long-term commitment. A great team can turn a small project into a cultural phenomenon.

The fifth principle is analyzing **scarcity and supply mechanics**. Scarcity determines how valuable an NFT can ultimately become. Projects with limited supply tend to hold stronger value as demand increases. But scarcity must be paired with actual demand—otherwise it becomes meaningless. Investors study supply size, rarity traits, trait distribution, scarcity tiers, and token-gated sub-communities within the collection. They also examine minting mechanisms, burn mechanisms, and any mechanisms that reduce supply over time. NFT supply should be aligned with the project's vision and user base.

The sixth principle involves evaluating **real adoption and usage**. Many NFT projects promise utility, but few deliver experiences people actually use. Investors look for NFTs that are integrated into virtual worlds, gaming ecosystems, membership structures, or digital identity systems. They evaluate how often holders engage with NFT features, attend events, claim rewards, or participate in governance. Real adoption often separates sustainable NFT ecosystems from speculative ones.

The seventh principle is **partnerships and integrations**. Successful NFT projects often partner with major brands, metaverse platforms, creators, gaming studios, or educational institutions. These partnerships expand visibility, increase utility, and build long-term adoption. Investors analyze partnership quality, frequency, and impact—not just hype announcements. Strong integrations signal a healthy ecosystem and future demand.

The eighth principle is studying **market positioning and differentiation**. Investors assess whether the NFT collection has a unique purpose, design, or ecosystem. Copycat collections are common and rarely gain long-term traction. Unique positioning—through art style, story, technology, or utility—creates defensibility. NFTs must stand for something, represent something, or unlock something that cannot be easily replicated.

Another essential factor is **liquidity and market behavior**. NFTs are less liquid than cryptocurrencies, meaning they can take longer to sell and have wider price swings. Investors evaluate historical trading volume, listing percentages, marketplace presence, floor price strength, and bidding activity. Healthy liquidity indicates strong demand. Weak liquidity suggests risk, even if the project looks promising.

Finally, professional investors look at **trajectory and sustainability**. Projects that deliver consistent updates, roadmap milestones, community events, and new innovations tend to appreciate in value over time. Projects that stagnate eventually decline. The NFT world is dynamic, and successful collections evolve with technology, culture, and community needs.

When you understand these evaluation principles, you stop viewing NFTs as pictures—and start seeing them as digital property, virtual brands, identity assets, and future income streams. By mastering this chapter, you gain the ability to identify NFT assets with real long-term potential while avoiding short-term speculation disguised as opportunity.

"The Gallery of Living Symbols"

Aiden met Nova at the entrance of a massive floating museum, its crystalline walls shimmering like a prism suspended above the clouds. "Welcome to the Gallery of Living Symbols," she said. "Inside this place, NFTs are not simply images. They are identities, communities, tools, and worlds."

Aiden stepped through the glass doors, and the interior expanded into a breathtaking landscape. The gallery wasn't arranged like a traditional museum. Instead, each NFT collection occupied its own immersive environment—an entire world built around the meaning, story, and community behind the art.

Nova guided him into the first chamber, where rows of glowing emblems floated like stars. Each emblem pulsed with a unique rhythm, and as Aiden reached out, he saw visions of utility unfold—access to private academies, membership in elite guilds, tools that unlocked productivity, and passes granting entry to exclusive events. "Utility," Nova said. "This is the heartbeat of value. NFTs that offer purpose endure. NFTs that offer nothing fade." They entered a circular hall bursting with energy. Thousands of avatars filled the space, debating, laughing, celebrating, sharing artwork, hosting events, and welcoming newcomers. The room's walls displayed real-time community activity—messages, collaborations, votes, and milestones. "A strong community keeps a project alive," Nova explained. "People give meaning to symbols. They build culture, defend value, and drive momentum." Aiden felt the community's power—its unity, passion, and identity. It was clear why certain NFTs thrived despite market volatility.

Next, Nova brought him into a chamber resembling an ancient temple. In the center was a single pedestal holding a timeless, iconic NFT glowing with profound intensity. It radiated cultural significance, history, and reverence. "Some NFTs," Nova said, "aren't just assets. They're cultural monuments." Aiden realized that certain collections represented movements, beliefs, and digital identity. They were valuable not only because of scarcity or utility, but because they became symbols recognized across the metaverse.

They then entered a workshop filled with holographic tools, brushes, and coding grids. Here, the founding teams of various NFT projects appeared as digital spirits working tirelessly—designing art, hosting community calls, releasing updates, building integrations, and improving utility. Nova said, "Teams determine destiny. Vision begins with them, but survival depends on execution." Aiden watched as one team refined its roadmap, another built new features, and another solved a technical issue in real time. He could see how leadership directly shaped value.

The next room contained a swirling landscape of floating NFTs—each orbiting according to its rarity. Some glowed brightly, rare and coveted. Others shined softly, representing more common traits. Nova explained the mechanics of scarcity, showing him how demand interacted with supply, how rarity traits influenced desirability, and how balanced distribution created stable value. "Scarcity without demand is meaningless," she said. "But scarcity paired with culture becomes priceless."

They moved into an amphitheater where partnerships came to life as animated scenes. Brands entered virtual worlds, NFT characters collaborated with gaming ecosystems, collections integrated with metaverse platforms, and creators licensed their artwork for digital and physical merchandise. "Partnerships expand universes," Nova said. "They multiply value." Aiden watched how each collaboration expanded reach, strengthened identity, and brought new users into the ecosystem.

The final chamber was dim and quiet. Abandoned NFTs floated silently—once hyped, now forgotten. Their colors were dull, their communities empty. "These," Nova said, "are the consequences of weak leadership, no utility, or lost narrative." Aiden felt a pang of sadness for them. But Nova placed a hand on his shoulder. "This is why knowledge matters. You will not choose blindly."

As they walked back toward the gallery entrance, Aiden looked at the living symbols around him—some glowing with new life, others with legendary history. NFTs were not pictures; they were digital worlds shaped by people, culture, technology, and purpose.

Nova turned to him. "If you learn to see what others ignore, you will find the NFTs that endure. And they will become pillars in your metaverse portfolio."

Aiden stepped into the light, feeling wiser, sharper, and more prepared than ever before. The gallery had shown him the truth: NFTs weren't just art—they were futures waiting to be chosen.

Chapter 6

Virtual Real Estate Mastery: How to Evaluate, Buy, Monetize, and Grow Profitable Digital Land in the Metaverse

Virtual real estate is one of the most exciting and misunderstood assets in the metaverse. For many investors, the idea of buying "land that isn't real" seems absurd—until they understand the economic principles that make digital property valuable, monetizable, and foundational to the Web3 economy. Digital land is not simply a product of imagination; it is programmable space, attention real estate, digital infrastructure, and the foundation for experiences, businesses, communities, and commerce. This chapter teaches the professional-level strategies for evaluating, purchasing, and monetizing virtual land across multiple metaverse platforms.

The first principle in understanding virtual real estate is recognizing that **digital land behaves like a hybrid of physical real estate and early-stage technology investing**. It has scarcity, location dynamics, rental potential, and demand cycles similar to physical land—but it also has adoption risk, update cycles, and scalability comparable to software. This makes digital real estate extremely powerful for early investors who understand trends. Each parcel is an opportunity to create income streams, build interactive worlds, host businesses, sell services, or position yourself at the center of growing digital communities.

The second principle is evaluating **platform strength and ecosystem health**, which determines long-term land value. A parcel of land in a failing platform is worthless. A parcel in a thriving, fast-growing world can appreciate exponentially. Investors study user activity, developer support, creator adoption, corporate partnerships, gaming integration, content tools, and community engagement. High-value land exists on platforms where people gather, socialize, transact, play, work, and build. Before buying any land, you must first evaluate the metaverse platform itself—its technology, roadmap, leadership, and cultural momentum.

The third principle is understanding **location dynamics**, which can dramatically influence land value. In the metaverse, "location" does not depend on physical geography but on digital foot traffic, proximity to major hubs, adjacency to popular creators, and closeness to business districts. Land near event arenas, marketplaces, spawn points, transportation hubs, or influencer-owned parcels tends to attract higher demand. Investors analyze heat maps, user flow data, event schedules, and social clustering to determine which areas have the strongest long-term potential. Just like in the physical world, location compounds value over time.

The fourth principle is evaluating **utility and build potential**. Unlike physical land, digital land can transform instantly. It can be a business one day, a gallery the next, a conference hall the next. Investors evaluate what can be built on the land: shops, rental spaces, games, training centers, classrooms, immersive experiences, event venues, or branded environments. The flexibility of digital land makes it extremely powerful for entrepreneurs who want to develop income-generating assets. The best parcels offer easy build tools, customizable features, and integration with creator economies.

The fifth principle involves understanding **monetization models**, which include digital rentals, advertising, hosting, selling virtual goods, launching digital businesses, selling naming rights, and revenue-sharing with creators. Virtual land monetization varies significantly by platform. In creator-focused worlds, landowners earn from renting build space. In gaming worlds, landowners earn from in-game utility. In event-driven worlds, landowners generate income by hosting concerts, workshops, or conferences. The more monetization pathways a platform offers, the more valuable land becomes. The sixth principle is analyzing **market cycles**

and timing, which heavily influence digital land opportunities. During hype cycles, land prices skyrocket as new users rush into virtual worlds. During consolidation phases, prices stabilize or dip—creating ideal buying opportunities. Smart investors avoid buying land at peak mania and instead accumulate during quieter periods when attention has shifted elsewhere. Just like physical real estate investing, timing matters. The early stages of a platform often offer the highest long-term upside if supported by strong fundamentals.

The seventh principle is understanding **scarcity and supply mechanics**. Some platforms offer fixed supply, while others expand land availability over time. A platform with infinite expansion dilutes value. A platform with controlled scarcity creates exclusivity and higher appreciation potential. Investors evaluate how supply is released, how land is minted, how expansions are managed, and whether scarcity aligns with demand. Scarcity without adoption is meaningless, but scarcity paired with a strong ecosystem becomes incredibly valuable.

The eighth principle is researching **creator economies and builder support**, which determine how vibrant a metaverse world becomes. A platform with strong building tools, low barriers to entry, educational resources, and monetization programs tends to attract developers and creators—leading to vibrant districts, events, experiences, and commerce. The best land investments occur in worlds where creators thrive because creators bring users, and users bring value.

Another important factor is evaluating **enterprise adoption**. Land near corporate headquarters, brand partnerships, or enterprise districts often gains long-term demand as companies build permanent digital presences. These zones become stable anchors for surrounding land value. Investors study which brands, influencers, and institutions are investing in each metaverse world to forecast where long-term attention will flow.

Finally, investors must develop **long-term land management strategies**, which include development plans, rental systems, upgrade cycles, event hosting schedules, and partnerships with creators or brands. Digital land is not a passive investment—it is an evolving asset that rewards active participation. The best investors treat land like a business, not a collectible.

By mastering these principles, you gain the ability to identify high-potential land, acquire it at the right time, build valuable experiences, and generate income streams inside virtual worlds. Digital real estate is not the future—it is the present.

And those who understand how to use it will shape the next generation of digital commerce.

"The City of Shifting Worlds"

Nova led Aiden through a glowing doorway that opened into a breathtaking landscape—a sprawling metropolis suspended in the sky. The city stretched endlessly in every direction, with floating islands connected by neon bridges, holographic marketplaces, towering event arenas, and shimmering residential towers. "Welcome," Nova said, "to the City of Shifting Worlds—the center of virtual real estate across the metaverse."

Aiden felt overwhelmed by the sheer scale. Everywhere he looked, creators built new structures, developers coded interactive spaces, and communities gathered in digital districts filled with life and motion. "This," Nova said, "is where land becomes possibility."

They began their journey in a thriving district filled with stores, galleries, and creator studios. The foot traffic was constant. Avatars browsed shops, attended classes, bought digital goods, and visited immersive experiences. "This land," Nova said, "is valuable because people gather here. Location in the metaverse is measured by activity, not geography." She showed Aiden how the platform mapped user flow, heat clusters, and event timing. Aiden could see why these parcels commanded high prices. Next, Nova teleported him to a deserted zone on the edge of the map. Abandoned structures floated in silence. "These were bought during a hype cycle," she said. "Buyers believed price momentum was the same as long-term demand. They were wrong." Aiden shivered as he walked through the ghost district. The emptiness felt heavy. "Real estate isn't valuable because it's scarce," Nova explained. "It's valuable because it's used."

They continued to a central plaza where a massive event arena glowed with energy. A virtual concert was about to start. Crowds gathered in anticipation. Vendors sold digital merchandise. Creators prepared live shows. "Event-centric land is extremely valuable," Nova said. "The more people gather, the more opportunities for monetization." As the concert began and the arena filled with thousands of avatars, Aiden felt the electricity of digital community at scale.

Nova then brought Aiden to a platform high above the city. Below them, holographic signs identified parcels owned by global brands, influencers, and DAOs. "Enterprise adoption," she said, "is a major driver of land value." Aiden watched as brand representatives built interactive experiences, corporate headquarters, and learning hubs. "Land near these anchors appreciates over time," she said. "Just like in the real world."

They teleported to a creator district where developers designed buildings with high-tech tools. Aiden watched as a creator constructed a floating café in real time. Another built a gaming arena. A third designed a training center. “Creator economies sustain metaverse cities,” Nova said. “The more creators a platform attracts, the more alive its worlds become.” Aiden saw how creator tools, education, and community support influenced land value and platform growth.

Next, Nova showed him land monetization firsthand. They entered a commercial zone where property owners rented space to creators, hosted paid workshops, ran subscription-based experience hubs, and sold virtual goods. Some had automated rental systems. Others offered customizable storefronts. “This is where land becomes business,” Nova said. “The income potential is limited only by imagination.”

They visited a platform's expansion zone where new land was being minted. Nova explained how supply mechanics impacted long-term value. “Some worlds expand endlessly,” she said. “Others protect scarcity. Investors must study each world carefully.” Aiden realized that understanding supply was essential for predicting appreciation.

Their last stop was a breathtaking floating island overlooking the entire metropolis. It was peaceful and untouched—a blank canvas. "This," Nova said, "is development land. You shape its destiny." She explained how investors built businesses, created events, partnered with creators, and developed long-term plans. "Digital land is not static," she said. "It is alive. And what you build determines its future."

Aiden looked down at the glowing city below. The shifting landscapes, bustling districts, and living ecosystems. He understood now: virtual real estate was more than land. It was opportunity. Creativity. Enterprise. Community. Innovation.

Nova turned to him. "You are ready to own a piece of a world," she said. "But more importantly—you are ready to shape it."

Aiden nodded. For the first time, he felt like he could build something lasting, something meaningful, something alive. And the City of Shifting Worlds would be the place where his vision began.

Chapter 7

Mastering DAO Investing: Governance Tokens, Treasury Power, Voting Rights, and Collective Wealth Creation

Decentralized Autonomous Organizations—DAOs—represent one of the most significant innovations in Web3. They transform organizations, investment groups, communities, and businesses into decentralized networks governed by their members. Instead of CEOs or boards making decisions, DAOs operate through tokenized voting, open proposals, collective treasury management, and transparent on-chain rules. For investors, DAOs provide opportunities to influence the future of digital platforms, earn rewards, shape governance, and hold tokens with long-term value. This chapter explains how professional investors evaluate DAO tokens and use them to build wealth and influence in the metaverse.

The first principle in DAO investing is understanding **governance power**, the central function of DAO tokens. Governance tokens allow holders to vote on proposals, platform updates, treasury decisions, partnerships, and economic strategies. Not all governance tokens are equal. High-value tokens grant meaningful influence; low-quality tokens offer votes that rarely matter or govern systems that lack direction. Investors analyze how much power governance provides, how often decisions occur, and whether governance influences real platform outcomes. Strong governance equals strong long-term value.

The second principle involves evaluating **treasury strength**, which represents the financial backbone of a DAO. The treasury is the pool of funds, resources, tokens, and assets controlled by the DAO membership. A large, well-managed treasury gives the DAO significant power—funding builders, launching initiatives, investing in startups, rewarding contributors, and powering long-term growth. Investors examine treasury size, diversification, liquidity, revenue sources, spending patterns, transparency, and runway. A strong treasury signals a durable DAO capable of thriving across multiple market cycles.

The third principle is analyzing **proposal quality**. DAOs with clear, thoughtful, well-structured proposals tend to be healthy, organized, and visionary. DAOs with chaotic or poorly written proposals often lack leadership or community alignment. Investors evaluate how proposals are created, how they are debated, how the community participates, and how quickly decisions are executed. A DAO with strong proposal structure signals professionalism and long-term value creation. The fourth principle is assessing **community participation**, which determines whether the DAO functions effectively or devolves into inactivity. Strong DAOs have active members contributing ideas, discussing proposals, building tools, hosting events, managing partnerships, and helping improve the platform. Weak DAOs have silent members, low voting turnout, and stagnant discussions. Investors track voting participation rates, community call attendance, and forum engagement to determine whether a DAO has a thriving membership or superficial activity.

The fifth principle involves studying **leadership dynamics**, even though DAOs are decentralized. Successful DAOs still require leadership—people who coordinate initiatives, mentor contributors, communicate with the community, and help guide the organization's direction. A DAO without informal or formal leadership tends to drift. Investors analyze how leadership emerges, whether leaders communicate transparently, and whether the community respects and follows them. Leadership strength often determines DAO longevity.

The sixth principle is evaluating **tokenomics**, including supply distribution, vesting schedules, inflation mechanics, and utility. DAO tokens must be designed to incentivize participation, reward contributors, and protect long-term value. Investors study whether token supply is concentrated in the hands of founders or evenly distributed among community members. They evaluate whether tokens offer staking rewards, access benefits, governance rights, or yield opportunities. Strong tokenomics create a sustainable governance economy; weak tokenomics destroy value over time.

The seventh principle involves analyzing **ecosystem impact and partnerships**. DAOs with strong partnerships, integrations, and collaborations tend to expand faster than isolated DAOs. Successful DAOs collaborate with gaming platforms, metaverse worlds, creator networks, DeFi protocols, or brands. These collaborations create new utility for DAO tokens and attract new members. Investors look for DAOs that operate like digital companies—producing value, launching products, and forming alliances.

The eighth principle is **risk management**, especially because DAOs face unique challenges. Governance attacks, proposal manipulation, treasury misallocation, regulatory uncertainty, and community conflict can destabilize DAOs. Smart investors evaluate whether a DAO has safeguards—quorum rules, security audits, financial oversight, and conflict resolution systems. DAOs without guardrails are vulnerable to hostile takeovers or poor decision-making.

Another major factor is studying **historical execution**. Promises do not matter; results do. Investors examine whether the DAO has executed past proposals successfully, met roadmap goals, grown its treasury, or delivered value to members. DAOs with a strong track record are far more likely to create long-term value.

Finally, investors evaluate **DAO purpose and mission**. A DAO that exists without a clear objective often collapses under apathy. A DAO with a powerful mission—whether it's building open metaverse tools, investing in digital startups, running virtual worlds, funding creators, or supporting communities—attracts long-term believers. Purpose drives culture. Culture drives value.

When you combine these principles, you gain the ability to identify DAOs capable of shaping industries, building digital economies, and creating collective wealth. DAO investing is not only about financial returns—it's about becoming part of a digital organization where your voice influences the future. And investors who understand how DAOs work gain access to one of the most powerful forces in Web3.

"The Council of Many Voices"

Nova led Aiden into a grand chamber suspended in the sky, its architecture a mix of ancient marble and futuristic crystal.

Hundreds of floating seats encircled a glowing central podium. Around the room, avatars gathered—builders, strategists, creators, investors, dreamers—all preparing for a DAO council meeting. "This," Nova said, "is where digital worlds are shaped."

Aiden felt the energy immediately. Voices buzzed with anticipation. The air vibrated with the weight of decision-making. "DAOs," Nova said, "are the beating heart of decentralized worlds. Decisions made here ripple across entire ecosystems."

They floated toward the center, where holograms displayed proposals—funding a new creator academy, launching a governance upgrade, building a virtual district, partnering with an AI startup. "These proposals," Nova said, "are the lifeblood of the DAO. They show where ideas are born, where conflicts arise, and where community vision turns into reality."

Aiden watched as the first proposal went live. Community members stepped forward, sharing arguments, discussing pros and cons. Some advocated passionately. Others questioned details. Everyone had a voice. "Voting," Nova whispered, "is power. Governance tokens are not symbols—they are keys."

He noticed that some members spoke with authority and clarity—leaders, even though no one had formally appointed them. “Leadership emerges naturally,” Nova explained. “Good leaders guide DAOs forward. Weak leaders let them drift.” Aiden could see the difference. Strong DAOs had active, engaged, organized contributors. Weak DAOs had confusion, silence, or conflict.

They stepped into a treasury vault—a colossal chamber filled with glowing orbs representing the DAO’s assets. Each orb pulsed with energy, showing the value stored within. “Treasury power determines longevity,” Nova said. “A strong treasury can fund growth for decades. A weak one collapses under pressure.” She showed Aiden how treasury funds were allocated, how proposals accessed resources, and how financial transparency kept members aligned.

Next, they visited the forum district—a swirling landscape of discussions, ideas, arguments, and debates. Aiden saw community members sharing strategies, proposing tools, organizing events, and building partnerships. Nova pointed to the activity. “A DAO thrives when its members care,” she said. “Without participation, even the most promising DAO dies.”

They flew to another chamber where tokenomics appeared as flowing streams of energy—showing how tokens were distributed, vested, staked, and used. “Token design shapes behavior,” she said. “Bad tokenomics create chaos. Good tokenomics create long-term alignment." Aiden saw how some tokens encouraged participation while others caused dilution and decline. Another portal opened, showing DAOs with strong partnerships—collaborating with metaverse worlds, brands, gaming ecosystems, artists, and DeFi protocols. "Partnerships expand the DAO's influence," Nova explained. "They create momentum." Aiden watched how these alliances opened new opportunities, increased member engagement, and strengthened the DAO's cultural relevance.

Then the chamber dimmed as Nova led him into a quiet hall filled with abandoned DAO artifacts—failed proposals, inactive discussion boards, empty vaults, obsolete tokens. "These," she said, "are DAOs that lacked vision, leadership, or participation. They remind us that decentralization is powerful—but fragile." Aiden felt the lesson deeply. A DAO wasn't guaranteed to thrive. It required structure, passion, and collective purpose.

Finally, they returned to the main chamber as a major vote began. Members raised their governance tokens, which glowed brightly as they cast their votes. The room lit up like a constellation. Aiden felt the incredible sense of unity—hundreds of voices shaping a shared future. "This," Nova said, "is the Council of Many Voices. It is where the metaverse becomes what its people choose."

Aiden watched in awe as the proposal passed. The DAO celebrated. A new world would be built. A new path would unfold. And he realized something powerful: investing in DAOs wasn't just about owning tokens—it was about belonging to something larger.

Nova looked at him. "Are you ready to take your place in a council like this?" Aiden nodded, feeling a sense of purpose he had never felt before. He was ready—not just to invest, but to shape the digital world alongside others.

Chapter 8

Mastering Digital Businesses in the Metaverse: Building, Acquiring, Automating, and Profiting From Virtual Companies

One of the most powerful and rapidly expanding opportunities in the metaverse is the creation and ownership of **digital businesses**—income-generating virtual companies that operate inside decentralized worlds. Unlike physical businesses, digital businesses require no inventory, no physical space, no employees, and no local regulations. They scale globally from day one, operate 24/7, and can be automated through smart contracts, AI, and digital workflows. Chapter 8 reveals how high-level Web3 entrepreneurs evaluate, build, and acquire profitable digital businesses inside metaverse platforms.

The first principle of metaverse entrepreneurship is understanding that **digital businesses function like programmable income streams**. They operate on virtual land, inside virtual malls, across gaming ecosystems, or within creator economies. These businesses sell virtual goods, host events, provide services, run experiences, offer education, manage rentals, or deliver entertainment. Their "operational rules" are written in smart contracts or automated systems, allowing them to run even while the owner is offline. This automation removes the friction of physical business ownership and creates scalable, low-cost profit engines.

The second principle is evaluating **demand and opportunity gaps** within a metaverse platform. Just as physical cities have underserved sectors, digital cities also require services: avatar customization studios, virtual fashion brands, event hosting venues, digital real estate agencies, virtual storefronts, game-based item shops, AI-powered learning academies, and more. Professional metaverse entrepreneurs study user behavior, platform culture, and creator ecosystems to identify gaps. The best digital businesses solve meaningful problems—helping creators, educating users, offering tools, or entertaining communities.

The third principle is understanding **monetization models**, which vary widely depending on the business type. Some businesses generate revenue through one-time sales of digital goods or NFTs. Others collect recurring payments through subscriptions, memberships, or premium upgrades. Some earn marketplace fees, ad revenue, sponsorship deals, or affiliate income. Others earn residual income through staking, royalties, event ticket sales, or partnership revenue. The most powerful metaverse businesses combine multiple revenue streams to stabilize income and build long-term brand value.

The fourth principle is assessing **platform selection**, which dramatically affects a business's success. Each metaverse world attracts different audiences. Some attract gamers, others creators, others educators, and others corporate users. Entrepreneurs choose platforms where their business type thrives. A virtual clothing brand does well in avatar-driven worlds. A virtual concert venue thrives in entertainment worlds. A real estate agency thrives in land-based worlds. Platform selection determines demand, scalability, and long-term brand strength.

The fifth principle is evaluating **creator tools and development capabilities**. Platforms with robust building tools, low-code development environments, integrations with AI, and accessible monetization systems allow digital businesses to scale rapidly. Entrepreneurs favor platforms with strong support, builder tutorials, developer grants, creator communities, and partnership programs. A platform that empowers creators is fertile soil for growing digital enterprises.

The sixth principle is understanding **branding and digital identity**, which matter even more in the metaverse than in the physical world. Digital businesses succeed when they create memorable visual identities, avatars, logos, storefront designs, and immersive brand experiences. Because the metaverse is built on visual immersion, branding becomes a core strategic asset. Strong brands attract loyal users, build trust, and increase the value of associated NFTs or digital goods.

The seventh principle involves building **automation systems**. Digital businesses thrive when workflows are automated. Web3 automation tools handle payment distribution, inventory updates, reward systems, customer onboarding, access control, event scheduling, and more. AI agents manage customer service, marketing, content creation, and operations. Smart contracts automate revenue flows. The more automated the business, the higher the margins.

The eighth principle is analyzing **scalability**. A physical business grows by hiring more staff or opening new locations. A digital business grows by copying code, duplicating experiences, selling more NFTs, licensing content, or expanding across multiple metaverse platforms. Scalability determines whether a business becomes a small venture or a global brand operating in multiple worlds simultaneously.

Another key principle is evaluating **community integration**. Successful digital businesses embed themselves inside metaverse communities. They host events, sponsor creators, collaborate with influencers, or form guilds. They reward early users, partner with DAOs, and participate in the social culture of the platform. Community integration drives adoption, loyalty, and long-term sustainability.

The tenth principle is understanding **exit strategies**. Digital businesses can be sold, licensed, franchised, or tokenized. Owners can create NFT-based ownership shares, allowing investors to buy fractional stakes. They can sell their business assets—land, code, IP, branding—on marketplaces. Metaverse businesses can even become DAOs where the community owns and governs the company. Exit strategies allow entrepreneurs to unlock value and scale their impact.

Digital entrepreneurship in the metaverse is not just about creating virtual shops or event spaces. It is about **building programmable economies**, automated income engines, and virtual brands that live across worlds. By mastering the principles in this chapter, investors gain the ability to create, buy, or scale digital businesses that operate beyond physical limitations—and prosper in the emerging Web3 economic landscape.

"The Entrepreneur of a World Without Walls"

Aiden followed Nova through a luminous archway that opened into a sprawling commercial district unlike anything he had ever seen. Neon signs flickered overhead, floating storefronts drifted like islands in the air, and crowds of avatars visited businesses of every shape and style. "Welcome," Nova said, "to the Marketplace of Infinite Dreams."

The first business they visited was a virtual fashion atelier, where creators designed holographic clothing that shimmered with animation. Customers tried on outfits instantly, their avatars transforming with each selection. "Digital fashion," Nova explained, "is a billion-dollar industry. People express identity here just as they do in the physical world." The designer waved at Aiden, proudly showing outfits that sold to thousands of users across multiple worlds.

They then entered a massive event hall filled with floating stages and glowing seating pods. A virtual conference was underway—guests from around the world attending digitally. "Event hosting is one of the most profitable digital businesses," Nova said. "No travel, no physical costs, unlimited scalability." Aiden watched speakers give immersive presentations, each enhanced by interactive visuals and gamified tools.

Next, Nova transported him to a quieter zone where entrepreneurs built AI-powered learning academies. Students practiced skills through holographic simulations. Teachers earned tokens for hosting classes. "Education thrives here," she said. "Anyone can become a teacher, student, or academy owner." Aiden imagined building a learning space of his own—where knowledge and creativity shaped an entirely new type of school.

They landed in a rental district where property owners leased shop spaces, studios, and event venues to creators. Each rental contract was automated through smart contracts. Payments arrived instantly. "This," Nova said, "is digital passive income." Aiden saw how one landlord earned thousands each month by renting out a few prime parcels.

In another zone, they visited a game-based business—a combat arena generating revenue through entry fees, tournaments, and rewards. Spectators bet on matches, creators sold skins, and players earned tokens. "Gamified businesses," Nova explained, "are among the fastest-growing opportunities." Aiden felt the energy of the arena—the roar of the digital crowd, the thrill of combat, the unpredictability of tournaments.

They moved into the Automation District where businesses ran entirely without human operators. Smart contracts managed inventory. AI agents welcomed customers. Automated workflows handled everything from advertising to customer support. “Here,” Nova said, “you see the true power of digital entrepreneurship: a business that runs itself.” Aiden studied the systems closely, fascinated by how simple scripts could generate endless revenue.

Next, they traveled to the Franchise Frontier—where brands licensed their digital stores across multiple worlds. Entrepreneurs bought ready-made businesses, duplicated them, and expanded across metaverses just like installing software. “Scalability,” Nova said, “is unlimited here.” Aiden saw how one brand owner had over 50 virtual locations generating income 24 hours a day.

Their final stop was a sanctuary-like rooftop overlooking the entire commercial district. From above, the city glowed like a constellation of opportunity. Nova waved her hand, and holograms of digital businesses appeared around them—restaurants, schools, lounges, arcades, studios, marketplaces, museums, and more. “Every business here,” she said, “was built by someone who saw possibility instead of limits.”

Aiden felt a surge of inspiration. For the first time, he understood that digital entrepreneurship wasn't just an investment strategy—it was an art form. A way of creating value, shaping culture, and building something that could live forever in a world without physical boundaries. Nova looked at him with knowing eyes. "You now see what most never understand," she said. "In the metaverse, businesses aren't confined by walls. They are limited only by imagination."

Aiden gazed at the city, ready to build something of his own—a business that could serve, inspire, and thrive in this boundless digital world.

Chapter 9

Risk Management & Protection Strategies: Safeguarding Your Metaverse Portfolio Against Volatility, Scams, Market Cycles, and Technological Failure

Mastering the art of risk management is the difference between surviving in the metaverse and thriving in it. While the opportunities for wealth creation are enormous, the risks are equally significant. The metaverse is a fast-moving frontier filled with innovations, experiments, and unknowns. Prices can rise explosively and collapse suddenly. New platforms emerge while others disappear. Scams, hacks, and exploits occur. Regulations shift. Technologies evolve. Market cycles form and break. In this dynamic ecosystem, the only path to long-term success is a strong, structured, intelligent approach to risk management. Chapter 9 reveals the professional-level systems used by Web3 portfolio managers to protect and grow digital wealth in the metaverse.

The first risk management principle is understanding **market volatility**, which is far more intense in Web3 than in traditional finance. Prices can swing by 10–30% in a single day. Entire sectors rise or fall based on narratives, announcements, or sentiment shifts. To manage volatility, investors diversify across asset classes, platforms, and risk levels. They avoid overexposure to single tokens or ecosystems. They use dollar-cost averaging during accumulation phases and avoid purchasing during euphoric spikes. Volatility can be profitable, but only if managed strategically.

The second principle is protecting yourself against **scams and fraudulent projects**, which remain widespread in early-stage digital economies. Professional investors analyze team credibility, verify smart contract code, check community transparency, and avoid tokens with unclear ownership. They stay away from guaranteed-return schemes, anonymous founders with no history, unrealistic claims, and projects with aggressive timelines. They use blockchain explorers to verify transactions and avoid suspicious wallets. Knowledge and skepticism are essential shields in the metaverse.

The third principle is defending your assets against **security threats**. Hacks, phishing attacks, malware, and social engineering are some of the most common ways investors lose funds. Professionals use hardware wallets, multi-signature systems, encrypted backups, burner wallets for testing, and strict security hygiene. They avoid clicking unknown links, signing unknown smart contracts, or connecting their main wallets to unverified apps. They use cold storage for long-term holdings and separate wallets for daily activity. Security is not optional—it is a core requirement of metaverse investing.

The fourth principle is preparing for **platform failure**. Not every metaverse platform survives. Some lose users. Some run out of funding. Some face regulatory issues. Others suffer technical collapse. Investors must assess platform longevity by evaluating developer strength, financial runway, adoption, ecosystem partnerships, and governance health. They avoid putting all assets into a single world. They buy land, NFTs, or tokens across multiple platforms to reduce the risk of catastrophic loss. Diversification across worlds is fundamental.

The fifth principle involves managing **liquidity risk**. Some NFT collections, virtual land assets, or small-cap tokens can take weeks or months to sell. Low liquidity increases price volatility and complicates exit strategies. Professional investors evaluate trading volume, listing ratios, marketplace depth, and buyer demand before acquiring assets. They avoid allocating excessive capital into illiquid assets unless they represent long-term conviction plays.

The sixth principle is understanding **regulatory risk**, especially as governments increasingly examine crypto, NFTs,

DAOs, and digital assets. Regulations can affect token classification, tax requirements, exchange operations, corporate integrations, and user rights. Investors stay informed, track regulatory sentiment, and diversify across decentralized and centralized ecosystems. They avoid assets that rely on regulatory loopholes or unsustainable models.

The seventh principle is protecting yourself from **psychological risk**—fear, greed, impatience, and emotional decision-making. Many investors buy at peaks and sell at bottoms because they react emotionally to price movements. Professionals develop long-term plans, set buying and selling rules, journal their decisions, and avoid impulsive trading. They understand market cycles and wait patiently during consolidation periods. Emotional discipline is as important as technical knowledge.

The eighth principle is mastering **portfolio rebalancing**, which protects gains and reduces exposure. As certain assets grow rapidly, they can become disproportionately large within your portfolio, increasing risk. Professionals rebalance periodically—taking profits from overextended assets and reallocating them into undervalued or long-term positions. Rebalancing transforms volatility into strategic growth.

The ninth principle is understanding **technological risk**. Smart contract vulnerabilities, bridge exploits, oracle failures, and code bugs can lead to catastrophic losses. Investors research audits, security practices, code transparency, and development maturity. They avoid interacting with unaudited protocols or high-risk contracts. They choose ecosystems that prioritize long-term reliability.

The tenth principle is preparing for **macro and market cycle risk**. Web3 markets move through predictable cycles—expansion, hype, correction, accumulation, and rebirth. Investors study cycle indicators, on-chain behavior, liquidity flows, global economic conditions, and narrative shifts. They avoid overextending during late bull markets and accumulate during early bear markets. Understanding cycles transforms fear into opportunity.

Finally, the eleventh principle is implementing **exit strategies and fail-safes**. Investors set predetermined profit targets, stop-loss thresholds, and emergency liquidity sources. They avoid tying up all capital in speculative assets. They maintain stablecoin reserves to capitalize on downturns. Exit strategies ensure that gains are protected and that losses never spiral out of control.

Risk management is not a defensive practice—it is the foundation of long-term wealth creation. Investors who master risk can survive the extreme volatility of the metaverse, capitalize on opportunities during downturns, and build resilient portfolios capable of thriving in any environment. This chapter equips you with the mental models and practical tools needed to protect your digital world.

"The Fortress of Falling Markets"

Nova led Aiden through a darkened forest where the trees flickered like blue fire. Ahead, a massive stone structure rose from the digital ground—a colossal fortress with shifting walls and glowing runes carved into its surface. "This," Nova said, "is the Fortress of Falling Markets. It protects those who understand risk and destroys those who ignore it."

As they approached, the gates opened on their own. Inside, Aiden stepped onto a bridge suspended above a swirling void. Ghostly images appeared beneath the transparent floor—investors panicking during crashes, losing everything to scams, or watching their assets vanish in platform failures. "These are lessons," Nova said softly. "Not warnings—truths."

The first chamber they entered was the Hall of Waves. Massive holographic price charts rose and fell like crashing oceans. Red waves towered above them, slamming into stone pillars. Blue waves surged in triumphant arcs. "Volatility," Nova said. "It terrifies the unprepared but rewards the disciplined." Aiden reached out and felt the force of the price waves. He understood now how dangerous the market could be—and how powerful it was for those who navigated it wisely.

They moved into the Chamber of Deception, where holographic figures disguised as friendly guides lured unsuspecting investors into traps. Projects with stolen artwork. Tokens with fake teams. Platforms with hidden codes. Aiden watched as avatars were drained of assets. "Scams evolve constantly," Nova said. "Your shield is knowledge. Your armor is skepticism." She handed him a glowing visor that revealed hidden dangers. When he looked through it, the scammers' illusions shattered instantly.

In the Chamber of Shadows, Aiden saw dark tendrils representing hacks and exploits creeping across the walls. Wallets drained. Smart contracts cracked. Bridges compromised. "Security failures," Nova said. "These shadows strike quickly." She showed him how hardware wallets glowed like shields, repelling attacks. Multi-signature vaults flickered like forcefields. She taught him the rituals of blockchain hygiene—cold storage, seed phrase protection, and smart contract caution.

Next was the Room of Fallen Platforms. Broken cities floated in midair—empty worlds that once thrived. Digital skyscrapers cracked. Abandoned plazas echoed with silence. "These platforms failed," Nova explained. "Poor leadership. Weak adoption. Unsustainable tokenomics." Aiden studied them carefully, absorbing the lessons hidden inside each ruined world.

They then stepped into the Chamber of Liquidity, where rivers of glowing energy represented trading volume. Some rivers flowed freely. Others dried up, trapping assets in stagnant pools. Nova said, "Liquidity determines your escape routes." She showed him how to test depth, evaluate volume, and avoid liquidity traps.

The Chamber of Governance Storms followed—where avatars argued in chaotic councils, proposals failed, and communities fractured. "Psychology," Nova said, "can be your greatest enemy." Aiden watched as fear spiked markets downward and greed pushed them too high. "Master yourself," she said, "and the market can never master you."

In the Chamber of Cycles, massive gears turned endlessly, representing bull markets, bear markets, accumulation phases, and explosions of growth. Nova explained how each cycle had signals, patterns, and opportunities. "Most fear the winter," she said. “But winter is where fortunes are built.” Aiden saw investors accumulating during downturns, only to rise with new strength in the next expansion.

Their final stop was the Vault of Preservation. Inside, glowing treasures floated in glass chambers—representing assets protected through strategy, discipline, and foresight. “These,” Nova said, “belong to those who respect risk.” She showed him rebalancing rituals, stablecoin reservoirs, profit-taking practices, and emergency exit paths.

As Aiden absorbed it all, the fortress began to glow. Walls strengthened. Doors sealed. The structure stood undefeatable. Nova turned to him. “With these principles, your portfolio becomes a fortress. Not to hide from the world—but to thrive within it.”

Aiden felt a deep sense of confidence. Risk no longer frightened him. It empowered him. He understood now that true strength in the metaverse didn’t come from chasing gains—it came from protecting them.

Nova smiled. “Now,” she said, “you are ready for the final chapter—the strategies that turn knowledge into generational digital wealth.”

Chapter 10

Long-Term Metaverse Wealth Strategies: Advanced Portfolio Design, Compounding Systems, and Generational Digital Asset Growth

Chapter 10 brings everything together. After mastering crypto analysis, NFT evaluation, land strategies, DAO governance, digital businesses, and risk management, you now possess the foundational tools to build real wealth inside the metaverse. But knowledge alone doesn't create financial independence. Wealth is produced through **long-term strategy**, **structured systems**, and **disciplined execution**. This chapter reveals how professional Web3 investors, digital asset funds, and metaverse entrepreneurs design portfolios not just for profit—but for generational growth.

The first principle of long-term metaverse wealth is understanding **portfolio architecture**, the intentional structure that determines your growth, risk tolerance, liquidity, and long-term potential. High-level investors structure their portfolios across multiple layers: foundational assets, growth assets, high-upside assets, cash-flow assets, and speculative positions. Foundational assets include major cryptocurrencies and blue-chip digital goods. Growth assets include mid-tier platforms, land, and expanding ecosystems. Cash-flow assets include digital businesses, rentals, or yield-generating tokens. Speculative assets include early-stage tokens and new metaverse projects. This layered approach ensures balance, resilience, and compounding potential.

The second principle is applying **time-based allocation**, where each asset has a strategic holding timeline. Long-term conviction assets—such as established blockchains, premium NFTs, or top-tier land—are held across cycles. Medium-term assets—such as young DAOs, mid-tier platforms, or new gaming worlds—are held through development phases. Short-term speculative assets are used strategically during narrative shifts. Time-based allocation prevents emotional decision-making and gives each asset type a role in your financial architecture.

The third principle is building **compounding systems**, which transform digital assets into long-term wealth engines. Compounding occurs through staking rewards, governance incentives, creator royalties, land rentals, subscription businesses, marketplace fees, yield farming, or automated smart contract income. Compounding systems allow your portfolio to grow even during flat or down markets. By reinvesting rewards strategically, you accelerate wealth accumulation exponentially. This is one of the most underrated strategies in metaverse investing—and one of the most powerful.

The fourth principle is strategic **liquidity management**. Long-term investors always keep part of their portfolio in stablecoins or low-volatility assets. This liquidity acts as ammunition during downturns, enabling investors to buy undervalued assets when the market is fearful. Liquidity is also a protective layer—covering unexpected needs or opportunities without forcing liquidation of long-term positions. Smart liquidity management prevents panic selling and preserves strategic flexibility.

The fifth principle is **cycle intelligence**, the ability to understand where the market stands within its natural rhythm. Web3 markets move through hype cycles, crashes, accumulation phases, and revival phases. Investors who master cycles gain unfair advantages. They accumulate during fear, expand during growth phases, protect gains during euphoria, and prepare for winter while others blindly chase momentum. Cycle intelligence is one of the most important factors separating long-term winners from short-term speculators.

The sixth principle is mastering **cross-world expansion**—building assets, businesses, and investments across multiple metaverse ecosystems. Wealthy investors never rely on a single world. They spread their presence across gaming, social, entertainment, creator, and decentralized identity platforms. Cross-world expansion multiplies exposure to future winners and protects against platform failures. It also creates synergies: a brand, NFT collection, or business built in one world can be replicated, licensed, or expanded into others.

The seventh principle is understanding **brand equity and digital reputation**, which become powerful wealth multipliers. In the metaverse, your identity as a creator, investor, landlord, builder, or business owner compounds in value. Reputation attracts partnerships, customers, opportunities, and community trust. Digital identity becomes a form of capital. Investors cultivate it intentionally through consistency, transparency, collaboration, and contribution to ecosystems.

The eighth principle is mastering **interoperable asset strategy**, preparing for a future where assets move seamlessly between worlds. High-level investors focus on assets with cross-chain capabilities, universal utility, or adaptable functionality. These assets are positioned for the long-term evolution of the metaverse—where worlds will become interconnected digital nations. The ninth principle involves implementing **wealth protection systems**, including smart contract insurance, multi-signature vaults, distributed hardware storage, regulatory awareness, and digital estate planning. Long-term investors prepare for unforeseen events. They protect their heirs' ability to inherit digital assets. They create legally recognized digital wills, automate transfers, or establish DAO-based inheritance systems. Generational wealth is not just about growth—it is about continuity.

The tenth principle is building **scalable digital empires**, where your assets reinforce each other. An NFT collection that drives traffic to your virtual business. A digital business that increases land value. A DAO membership that strengthens your brand. A set of cross-chain tokens that fuel your operations. Wealthy investors design interconnected ecosystems, not isolated holdings.

Finally, the eleventh principle is embracing a **builder mindset**, not just an investor mindset. The greatest fortunes in the metaverse will be made by people who create value—new experiences, digital products, businesses, infrastructure, communities, and systems. Investors who also build gain exponential leverage, influence, and income potential. The metaverse rewards those who combine innovation with ownership.

Long-term metaverse wealth is not about timing the market—but about creating systems that survive every cycle. It is about building, owning, compounding, and evolving with the digital world. By mastering the principles in this chapter, you gain the ability to create generational digital wealth—wealth that expands across worlds, platforms, economic cycles, and future innovations.

"The Architect of Tomorrow"

Aiden and Nova stood on a balcony overlooking a breathtaking digital landscape—a fusion of every world he had explored so far. Floating cities, neon marketplaces, towering DAOs, bustling creator hubs, sprawling lands, and glowing energy grids filled the horizon. "This," Nova said, "is the Metaverse of Many Futures."

Aiden felt a sense of completion—and beginning. Everything he had learned had prepared him for this moment.

Nova led him into a grand structure shaped like a fractal pyramid. Inside, glowing pillars represented the core of long-term wealth: architecture, cycles, compounding, and legacy. "Today," she said, "you become not just an investor—but an architect of tomorrow."

The first chamber was filled with layered models of portfolios suspended in midair. Each portfolio had rings representing foundational assets, growth zones, cash-flow engines, and speculative edges. "Portfolio architecture," Nova explained, "is the blueprint of resilience. Each layer supports the next." Aiden touched one model—it expanded like a galaxy, revealing cross-world token flows, revenue lines, and risk buffers.

The second chamber shifted into a timeline of the future. Assets aged. Markets cycled. Trends emerged. Early-stage tokens matured into major ecosystems. Once-hot projects faded. "Time shapes everything," Nova said. "Assign each asset a destiny before you buy it." Aiden watched his own imaginary portfolio play out across decades—some assets held through cycles, others harvested at peaks, others divested early.

In the Chamber of Compounding, rivers of light flowed into pools that grew exponentially. Each pool represented staking rewards, rentals, royalties, automation, or yield streams. "Compounding," Nova said, "is the silent builder of empires." Aiden watched as small streams turned into roaring waterfalls as they reinvested themselves endlessly.

Next, they entered the Chamber of Liquidity—a massive reservoir of glowing stable energy. "Liquidity is strength," Nova said. "It gives you clarity during storms." Aiden realized that every great investor carried reserves—not out of fear, but out of readiness. In the Chamber of Cycles, enormous gears rotated—each representing a phase of the market. Bulls. Bears. Accumulation. Mania. Collapse. Rebirth. Nova guided him through each one. “Cycles repeat,” she said. “Those who study them write their own future.”

The sixth chamber showed the Strategy of Many Worlds—holograms of different metaverses expanding, merging, or diverging. Aiden saw entrepreneurs running businesses across multiple worlds. “Never anchor yourself to one destiny,” Nova said. “Expand. Evolve. Spread your presence.”

Then came the Chamber of Reputation. Digital avatars glowed brighter or dimmer based on their actions. Builders shined like suns. Scammers faded into shadow. Collaborators pulsed with community energy. Nova said, “Your digital identity is your legacy. Guard it. Grow it. Honor it.”

They entered the Chamber of Interoperability next, where assets traveled through portals connecting worlds. Swords became skins. Skins became access passes. Tokens fueled tools. Property became multi-world headquarters. “The future,” Nova said, “belongs to assets that move freely.”

The ninth chamber revealed glowing vaults for wealth protection: multi-signature safes, smart contract insurance, distributed storage, legal wills, and inheritance protocols. “Wealth means nothing,” she said, “if it cannot survive you.”

Finally, they entered the greatest chamber—the Chamber of Creation. Here, holograms of future worlds shimmered in seed form. New schools. New businesses. New DAOs. New universes. “Builders,” Nova said, “ shape reality itself. Invest, yes—but also create. The metaverse grows through the dreams of its pioneers.”

Aiden stood at the center of the chamber as the worlds around him pulsed with possibility. He realized now that wealth was not a destination. It was something built through intention, discipline, vision, and creativity.

Nova stepped forward and placed a glowing architect’s prism in his hands. “This,” she said, “is your key to the future. With it, you may build worlds. The next era begins with you.”

Aiden looked out into the expanding universe of digital possibility. He felt ready—not just to invest, but to build an empire that would outlive him.

And as he walked forward into the bright horizon of infinite worlds, he finally understood his true role:

Not a trader. Not a collector. Not even an investor.

He was an architect of the metaverse.

Epilogue

"The New Frontier of Human Potential"

The metaverse is no longer a distant horizon, a science-fiction concept, or a bold prediction whispered among technologists. It is here, expanding, evolving, and redefining how humans interact, create, learn, trade, collaborate, and build wealth. As you arrive at the end of Book 10—and the culmination of the entire Metaverse Masterclass series—you now carry a level of understanding that most of the world does not yet possess. You have traveled through ten volumes that each reveal a different dimension of Web3: from the fundamentals of virtual worlds to the complexities of NFTs, platforms, decentralized identity, digital real estate, Web3 careers, DAO governance, digital businesses, and advanced investment strategy. You are no longer a newcomer or an observer. You are a digital pioneer stepping into an era that will redefine human potential.

This epilogue is more than a closing chapter. It is a reorientation of your vision, an invitation to step forward boldly, and a reminder that the metaverse revolution is still in its earliest stage. Despite the headlines declaring cycles of enthusiasm and correction, the underlying transformation continues to accelerate. Every year, millions of new users join decentralized platforms, creators launch new virtual businesses, global brands establish headquarters in digital worlds, and entire economies emerge from code. The future is being built in real time, and you now understand how to navigate it with clarity and mastery.

As you move forward, the most important truth to carry with you is this: **the metaverse rewards the creators, builders, strategists, and investors who design the future rather than wait for it.** You have learned how digital assets grow in value, how ecosystems expand, how compounding systems operate, how communities govern, and how digital businesses operate without walls or physical constraints. You have learned to analyze platforms, evaluate opportunities, protect capital, see cycles, and build intelligent strategies that transcend hype. Most people interact with the metaverse casually, but you now understand it architecturally. You see the mechanics beneath the experience, the economics beneath the visuals, the psychology beneath the markets, and the long-term opportunity beneath the temporary noise.

With this knowledge, the question becomes: **what will you build?** Some will build digital businesses that serve millions. Some will create virtual experiences that become landmarks. Some will develop communities that grow into powerful DAOs. Some will curate portfolios that appreciate across decades. Some will create art, fashion, games, tools, education, or cultural movements. And some will build the infrastructure that powers entire worlds.

The metaverse is not one destiny—it is a wide-open canvas waiting for visionaries. Unlike the physical world, where land and opportunity are limited by geography, politics, and resources, the metaverse expands with human imagination. Every new builder adds another layer of possibility. Every new world expands the ecosystem. Every new asset, business, or tool creates more opportunity for others. This compounding expansion is what makes the metaverse the most scalable frontier in human history.

But with great opportunity comes responsibility. You must remain grounded, informed, secure, and strategic. Market cycles will come and go. Platforms will rise and fall. Technologies will advance and evolve. Nothing in Web3 remains static. However, the principles you have learned throughout this series will guide you regardless of how the landscape changes. When new worlds emerge, you will know how to evaluate them. When new asset classes appear, you will understand how to allocate. When new risks arise, you will know how to protect yourself. When new opportunities present themselves, you will recognize them instantly. The metaverse belongs to the bold—but it rewards the disciplined. It belongs to the dreamers—but it rewards those who build consistently. It belongs to everyone—but it especially rewards those who learn faster, think deeper, collaborate smarter, and create value for others.

As the final reflection of this Masterclass, remember this truth: **we are living through the greatest transfer of creative power in human history.** For the first time, digital identity, ownership, creativity, and commerce blend into a unified landscape where anyone, anywhere, with nothing but a computer or headset, can build something that becomes globally significant. No gatekeepers. No borders. No limits. This is the democratization of creation—and you are now one of its architects.

The greatest pioneers of the metaverse will not be the corporations but the individuals who understand it deeply and act consistently. You are now part of the first generation capable of building an entire digital legacy—one that can not only survive across cycles, but live across worlds. As you close this final chapter, know that the metaverse is not just the future. It is a journey you are now fully equipped to navigate, shape, and lead.

The worlds ahead are vast. The opportunities are limitless. The only question left is: **what legacy will you create inside the metaverse?**

www.ingramcontent.com/pod-product-compliance
Lightning Source LLC
LaVergne TN
LVHW022010200926
848481LV00007B/2313
* 9 7 9 8 2 9 5 4 9 1 3 2 0 *